GETTING IN TOUCH
WITH YOUR INNER BITCH

GETTING IN TOUCH WITH YOUR INNER BITCH

Don't pretend you don't know what I'm talking about...

ELIZABETH HILTS

SOURCEBOOKS HYSTERIA™
An Imprint of Sourcebooks, Inc.®
NAPERVILLE, ILLINOIS

Published by Sourcebooks, Inc.
P.O. Box 4410, Naperville, Illinois 60567-4410
(630) 961-3900
FAX: (630) 961-2168
www.sourcebooks.com

Library of Congress Cataloging-in-Publication Data

Hilts, Elizabeth.
 Getting in touch with your inner bitch : now bitchier than
 ever / by Elizabeth Hilts.-- 2nd ed.
     p. cm.
 ISBN 1-4022-0308-X (alk. paper)
 1. Women--Humor. I. Title.
 PN6231.W6H54 2004
 305.4'02'02--dc22

                                        2004013183

         Printed and bound in the United States of America
              VP 10 9 8 7 6 5 4 3 2

This book is for my daughter, Shannon Hillory Hector, whose insight and assistance were essential elements in its completion; my granddaughter, Cassidy Elizabeth Singleton, who is continuing the fine family tradition of being a strong female; my husband, Neil Swanson, for being my safe harbor and for making me laugh more (and harder) than any other human being; and for my father, Robert Gifford Hilts, whom I still miss every day.

✓ COULD YOU TAKE
ON MORE WORK
WITHOUT A RAISE
OR A NEW title?

✓ I'D LIKE YOU TO
CALL MORE OFTEN.

✓ WOULD YOU MAKE
12 DOZEN COOKIES
FOR THE BAKE
SALE... SORRY it's
SUCH SHORT NOTICE.

Acknowledgments

I would like to offer special thanks to the women who keep me honest, provide the support I need to continue discovering the power of my Inner Bitch, and make me laugh out loud: Dawn Collins, Laura Fedele, Aida Little, Elaine Osowski, Ingrida Perri, and Felicia Moreland Robinson.

Thank you to all the people who played a part in making this book happen in the first place: Jim Motavalli (who believed in me long before I believed in myself); Mary Ann Masarech; Karen Drena; Piper Machette; my fairy godmother, Jocelyn K. Moreland; David Robinson; Jeff Yoder; and Mace Norwood, who was right all those years ago.

My agent, Tom Connor, provided invaluable guidance and clarity in the process of finding a home for the Inner Bitch. It continues to be a pleasure to share this adventure with him.

Thanks to Sarah Waite and Lysbeth Guillorn for research and editing the first edition and to Susie Benton for her assistance with this version; to the incomparable Nicole Hollander for creating the cover and, along with Marian Henley and Mary Lawton, the cartoons that still illustrate the absurdities of women's everyday life.

Very special thanks to Deborah Werksman for her insistence on bringing the Inner Bitch to the world.

And a big shout out to all the women and men who "get" the Inner Bitch.

contents

"WE HAD a LOT IN COMMON. I LOVED HIM. AND HE LOVED HIM."

—SHELLEY WINTERS

STOOD UP; WISED UP

Let me take a few moments to explain why I wrote this book.

It started with an article, "Get in Touch with Your Inner Bitch," published in Hysteria, the now-defunct humor magazine for women.

The magazine came out, a radio personality saw the article and called me for an interview, and suddenly I was deemed the Expert on the Inner Bitch.

Well, I am. But before I became the Expert on Her, I was an expert on the topic of Toxic Niceness. I was trained from the day of my birth in the ways of being Nice. The first thing my mother ever said to me was, "Elizabeth, behave."

And I tried. Honestly. I attempted to be a paragon of Niceness—a Melanie Wilkes, a Beth (from *Little Women*—or was it Amy?), a Nancy Drew. I memorized the names of the most toxic family, the Nicelys—Act, Speak, Sit, Think, even Dress.

Speak Nicely was tough. I tried to keep my voice low and well modulated. When that didn't work, I pushed it a full octave higher, which forced me to whisper. I thought I sounded sweet. Everyone else thought I had laryngitis.

Dress Nicely nearly pushed me to the edge. The first clue that this goal was going to prove problematic involved those little anklet socks with lace trim—which inevitably ended up creeping down into my Mary Janes and lodging in a tattered, mysteriously grimy mass under my heel. Not the neat, well–turned out effect my mother hoped for and which my peers pulled off with no tugging, yanking, or discernable effort whatsoever. Add in my flyaway hair, my tendency to get banged up while indulging in my passion for climbing trees, plus my heartfelt desire to wear jeans and a T-shirt whenever possible and the result fell far short of the Dress Nicely goal. When I began blossoming into womanhood it was even more challenging. Dress Nicely, when I wanted halter tops. Décolletage (non-existent, in my case)! Spandex!

But in the end, it was old Act Nicely that was the most toxic of the Nicelys for me. There was so much pressure to "behave"—which was code for putting on a pleasing demeanor. Not just from the adults in my life—who I'm certain believed they had my best interests in mind—but also from my girlfriends.

It's somewhat alarming to remember how many of my little girl friends were prone to sudden outbursts of the most damaging slogan for Toxic Niceness in existence—"Sugar and spice and everything NICE, that's what little girls are made of"—at the oddest moments. For instance, when I was pressing my case for a rousing game of touch football instead of going inside to play with their "Dolls of Many Lands" collection, the girls I knew would put their little hands on their hips, sashay up to well within hearing range and hiss those thirteen words in a menacing sing-song. It wasn't much of an argument, really. Nor were they exhibiting the niceness they advocated. "Nice," as was so often the case, meant acquiescence and it was clear that my next move was capitulation. I'd follow them inside where the "play" consisted mostly of gazing in mute admiration at impossibly statuesque and glamorous icons of womanhood while trying to ignore the gleeful hoots and hollers of the neighborhood lads.

At the same time, I noticed that those same boys seemed to have a built-in excuse for acting in ways that didn't fit into any definition of nice. You may have heard this magic phrase—"Boys will be boys."

It got even worse as we progressed to our preteen years. Along with the onslaught of puberty came a veritable tidal wave of advice on the best way to catch a boy. Never mind that the objects of all that energy were relatively oblivious to our wiles. Or that, frankly, the pool of potential Prince Charmings was, for the most part, anything but charming. Our entire focus was on interpreting the behavior of this exotic species and applying a scholarly approach to the best methods for capturing their attention and adoration.

While there were many mysteries inherent in attaining the coveted role of "someone's girlfriend," the consensus seemed to be that "being nice" was vital. "Nice" seemed to have taken on the added dimension of playing dumb, which manifested itself in giggling at nearly every word a boy said. Not laughing, giggling. It went without saying that challenging boys in any way—on the playing field (which we studiously avoided), in the classroom, when they made some ridiculous statement—was completely forbidden. At the same time, there was an almost intuitive understanding that one could be too Nice, which apparently had something to do with not opening one's mouth during a kiss.

At that point my training took on a whole new level of intensity. When I laughed too loud or when I actually said the things I knew we were all thinking, my girlfriends would say, "Stop making a spectacle of yourself!"

If extreme discretion was called for, they would nudge my arm and hiss, "Liiiiiz!" It almost made me long for the old "Dolls of Many Lands" days.

In private, they shrieked with laughter as they recounted the story of my latest outrageous behavior.

All the while, however, lurking just under the anxious surface of Niceness was our awareness of a basic, fearsome truth: it was the bitches who got all the good stuff. I mean, Scarlett O'Hara was the star of the movie, wasn't she? And she got the sequel. Melanie may have had

Ashley, but who wanted Ashley? Anyone with eyes could see that Ashley was—Ashley.

But I continued to try to force myself inside a sort of Niceness suit in hopes that someday it would prove to be a comfortable fit. Eventually, I manifested all the Niceness I could, bending over backwards to be agreeable, helpful, thoughtful, adoring, and adorable—in other words, a complete doormat.

Until IT happened. The event that finally made me see that Niceness could be toxic.

The Moment of Truth

IT had to do with a man. In my case, that phrase can be followed with the addendum, "of course." I used to find this an acutely embarrassing story, but that was before I really understood how debilitating the effects of Toxic Niceness are and how important sharing these experiences is in overcoming this epidemic. Here's what happened: I got stood up.

Yes. Left sitting in my living room on a Saturday night. After I'd tried on and rejected five different (fabulous) outfits. I called his house, got his machine. Left a message. "Hi, it's nearly 9:00. You must be running late. See you when you get here." 9:15, 9:45. I went upstairs at 10:30, took off my makeup, and got into bed, where I spent a sleepless night tossing and turning from concern to anger and back again all night.

"Maybe he had an accident?" I worried.

"He better have broken his jaw and both hands, complicated by total amnesia," a little voice inside my head responded.

"Oh. My. God! He could be lying in a ditch somewhere! Maybe I should go look for him."

"Maybe you'd better figure out once and for all if it's 'lying in a ditch' or just plain 'lying'—which seems like a better use of your time and energy. He's a lying liar is what he is. Forget him!"

He called the next day and actually said, "Something came up. You understand, don't you?"

Of course I did. I understood completely. He had a better offer and she was, undoubtedly, so much Nicer— or something—than I ever could be. But I forgave him anyway because he was really cute, and I really liked him. Mostly, however, because no one likes a bitch. How could a Nice Girl like me stay angry? He asked for another chance and I gave it to him.

You know it had to happen again. And this time, I went ballistic! I called his answering machine, ranting and raving until the tape ran out. Then I called back to yell some more. Finally, on the third go-round, I was all yelled out and the old training kicked in. "I'm really sorry, but I am really hurt," I whispered hoarsely into the phone. "Please call me."

Now that's embarrassing! I can't believe it myself. I apologized! I told his answering machine I was hurt! I wasn't hurt, I was furious! But, you know, he was cute, and I thought I could, maybe, really like him, and he'd never treat me so badly if he knew what a Nice Girl I was.

Right. The truth is, he'd never have treated me so badly if he knew what a bitch I could be. If I had been in touch with my Inner Bitch at that point, I would have called him on his disrespectful shenanigans immediately. I certainly wouldn't have spent an entire night wondering what failing on my part could have explained his complete lack of common courtesy and I never would have given him a second chance.

However, it took this incident to get me in touch with my Inner Bitch, and when I realized what I'd done, I decided right then and there that it was time to give up Toxic Niceness. It was time to emulate the bitches of the world. I would, as my mother would say, take a page from their book.

But there was no book.

Until now.

"NO WOMAN IS ALL SWEETNESS."

—MME. RÉCAMIER

CHAPTER ONE

TOXIC NICENESS

What is this mysterious malady that drives us to self-defeating behavior? Some people call this syndrome by different names: the "disease to please," co-dependency, nurturing.

The bottom line is this: when we suffer from Toxic Niceness, everyone else in our lives gets more out of our efforts than we do.

Our menfolk get to actually relax after work and on weekends while we take care of the laundry, the house-keeping, the grocery shopping, the thousand and one little things that have to be done to ensure that some degree of order can be maintained.

Our children get all of those benefits plus chauffeur services, tutoring, a live-in personal assistant who makes sure that the library books are returned on time and every conceivable craft supply they might need for school projects is in stock.

Our friends get a shoulder to cry on, a sympathetic ear, assistance with thankless tasks like pet-sitting, closet clearing, the removal of the mountain of belongings left behind by a recently absconding ex.

Our coworkers get someone who can be relied on to pick up an endless supply of slack so they can actually leave at 5:30 every night. Our employers get a dedicated worker who always gives 110 percent without asking for so much as a cost-of-living increase. Our direct reports get someone to take on all the effort involved in meeting demands for increased productivity without increased resources.

None of this is terrible and much of it is actually quite fulfilling. Except that Toxic Niceness is, by definition, a good thing taken to the extreme.

When we live with Toxic Niceness, we live on the giving end of a one-way street. Even when offers of reciprocation are made, those of us who suffer from Toxic Niceness feel honor-bound to refuse them.

The fact that you are reading this is proof that you are willing to consider letting go of Toxic Niceness. Are you a long-time sufferer of the syndrome? Ask yourself these questions:

1. Have you ever wanted to give someone a piece of your mind and eaten a piece of cake instead?
2. How about the whole cake?
3. Have the words, "I don't know what came over me!" ever sprung from your lips?
4. Have you ever refused an invitation because you were hoping that your latest love interest would finally ask you out for Saturday night?

5. Have you ever sat at home alone on Saturday night because he never called?
6. Have you ever said "yes" when you meant "I don't think so?"
7. Do you apologize for walking into someone else's office to ask a perfectly legitimate business-related question?
8. Have you ever worn a bridesmaid's dress with spaghetti straps?

If you answered yes to any of these questions, it's a sure thing that you're using too much sugar. But all is not lost—take heart. Toxic Niceness need not be a problem any longer.

Read on. Your Inner Bitch awaits you.

SYLVIA
by Nicole Hollander

"UNTIL YOU'VE LOST YOUR REPUTATION, YOU NEVER REALIZE WHAT A BURDEN IT WAS, OR WHAT FREEDOM REALLY IS."

—MARGARET MITCHELL

CHAPTER TWO

MEET YOUR INNER BITCH

There is a powerful and integral part of each of us that has until now gone unrecognized, its energy largely untapped. Years of repression have sent this aspect of ourselves into hiding in the nooks and crannies of our souls. Because we misunderstand it, we do all we can to keep it in the dark where we believe it belongs.

It is the Inner Bitch. Don't pretend you don't know what I'm talking about.

We all know Her. She floats constantly just under the surface of our consciousness and our culture. She is a part of ourselves that is smart, confident, dignified, and knows what she wants. She tells us not to settle for less. The Inner Bitch is like an early warning system in the battle for self-esteem and dignity, alerting us when we are about to embark on self-defeating behavior.

What the Inner Bitch is not is destructive. She is not stupid, mean, humorless, or abusive to Herself or others.

Oh, and She doesn't hate men or blame them for...well, anything.

The Inner Bitch does not engage in petty arguments, even for sport. Why bother? Though She is perfectly capable of a witty comeback along the lines of "I'll try being nicer if you'll try being smarter."

The Inner Bitch never enters into a battle of wits with an unarmed opponent. And She is never afraid to say, "Screw 'em if they can't take a joke."

I hold this truth to be self-evident: by getting in touch with our Inner Bitch, we are free to tap into Her power and energy for our own higher purposes.

If we ignore Her, we risk having Her run amok when the pressure of being Nice grows too strong. We've all seen it happen; it's not a pretty sight.

When we don't acknowledge our Inner Bitch, we get pimples. Or we get fat. Or too thin, controlling, manipulative, whiny, weepy, or hysterical. We don't insist on practicing safe sex.

None of this is productive. Some of it is downright dangerous.

How do we put an end to these self-defeating behaviors, particularly after a lifetime of Toxic Niceness?

All it takes is one short phrase:

"I DON'T THINK SO."

We all think it. But we bat it away like a pesky little gnat. "That's not nice," we think. But, oh, the price we pay.

You may be asking yourself, "But can I be nice without being toxic?"

Certainly you can! In fact, being in touch with your Inner Bitch actually helps you to be truly nice. There is a world of difference between being nice and being Nice.

Your Inner Bitch does not want you to be mean. She wants you to be firm. She wants you to be reasonable. And She wants you to be kind. Particularly to yourself.

GETTING TO "I DON'T THINK SO"

Give it a shot. Start out with small increments. Think of a situation in your life where it might be applicable. For example:

- Your twenty-two-year-old daughter wants to move into her old bedroom, rent–free, with her lover and his motorcycle.

  You say: "I don't think so."

- The man you've been dating for a month demands, in a fit of jealousy, that you cancel a dinner meeting with an important client.

  Your response: "I don't think so."

- Your mother wants you to meet the son of her bridge partner. "Just a little dinner, darling. We've made reservations for you at the Four Seasons after the theater."

  You smile: "Mom, I don't think so."

- Your boss strongly suggests that you invest your year-end bonus in his cousin's latest venture.

You: "I don't think so."

SAYING LESS, MEANING MORE

"I don't think so" has come under some heavy criticism from pundits and malcontents. They believe that the phrase is wimpy, annoying, and ultimately ineffective because it's perceived as "nagging."

I don't think so.

Look at the power in those four simple words! No one can mistake their meaning and arguing against the phrase is futile—how can anyone claim that you do think so if you say you don't think so? Particularly in the earliest stages of getting in touch, being able to respond to obnoxious requests and suggestions with "I don't think so" is incredibly empowering.

It's gentle. It's polite. At the same time, it's strong, firm, and indisputable.

The best thing about "I don't think so" is that it can be used at any time during a conversation. If you catch yourself sliding into Toxic Niceness, it's very easy to break the fall. And if you forget to say it, don't worry— the opportunity is guaranteed to come up again.

SAYING MORE

Naturally, there are times when "I don't think so" isn't enough. It's a base upon which to build, to make a sort of verbal sundae. Heap on as many toppings as you like.

- When a friend calls you at work—for the fifth time today—asking if you have time to talk: "I don't think so. Unless, of course, you promise to support me after I get the boot."
- When the head of the bake sale committee asks you the night before the sale to make a few dozen more of "your wonderful hand decorated cupcakes because they always sell so well"—"I don't think so, but I'll gladly show you how to make them before the next event."
- When a friend asks to borrow your great-grand-mother's diamond earrings because they'll look great with her new outfit—"I don't think so, but you're welcome to the cubic zirconia copies I had made."
- When the pushy saleswoman urges you to actually buy the outrageous print ensemble that just happens to match the outfit she's wearing—"I don't think that's a good color for me." You know it's multi-colored, she's knows it's multi-colored, and your point will be made.
- When the guy you've dated twice wants you to invite him in at the end of the night—"I don't think I'm ready for that."

Then there are those cases that require a certain delicacy combined with an ability to think on your feet:

- You are at a party talking with ten of your closest personal acquaintances. A friend of a friend introduces himself to you and says, "Do you know that Jim told me you're the perfect woman for me?"—"I don't think so, but hum a few bars."

You see, the phrase is polite and reasonable, never cruel, and not hard to say. Try different tones of voice. Give it a musing tone, or try putting the emphasis on different words: I don't think so. I don't think so.

I THINK I'D LIKE
TO BE LESS OF A
SWEETIE PIE
AND MORE
OF A
BITCH.

"YOU ONLY START BEING CALLED BITCH WHEN YOU BECOME SUCCESSFUL."

—JUDITH REGAN

CHAPTER THREE

THE PR PROBLEM

Some of us may have a problem claiming the term "bitch" for ourselves. We may believe that to do so would affirm the negative image assertive women have borne for years. To wit: if we say what we really think, we must be a bitch.

What causes this dynamic?

This question could keep sociologists and theorists busy for years, perhaps decades. That's fine. They need some way to justify the grant money. The simple truth is this: the true cause of the PR problem for the Inner Bitch is fear of being called a bitch.

After all, bitch is also a word that's synonymous with complaining, usually about something inconsequential or petty, right? "Bitch, bitch, bitch," is usually a retort akin to "waah, waah, waah," and the desirable result is that who-ever is doing the complaining will quit their whining.

This is becoming less of an issue, of course. Entire media empires are dedicated to promoting assertive self-expression and letting go of Toxic Niceness and its many pseudonyms. Women are increasingly proud of feeling a little bit like outlaws and are actually being rewarded for making bold moves. "Bitch" has, increasingly, become a word that conveys a certain level of respect and affection when referring to strong, outspoken women.

But that word. That word is just so…oh, I don't know, direct? In your face? And I get that to a degree. After all, I've experienced being called a bitch in the negative sense of the word…well, let's just say often.

Let's take a close look at this issue.

What exactly is the problem here? When we get labeled "bitch" are we really behaving badly? Or are we just going too fast, getting too far ahead, breaking out of our designated niche?

"Bitch" has much more history as a weapon against uppity women than as a term of wry affection and recognition. Calling us "bitch" puts us on notice that it is time to beat a hasty retreat to Toxic Niceness.

All I can say is, "I don't think so."

While it's tempting to point fingers and blame only men for using the word against us, that's just not true. Women use the word "bitch" as a weapon—usually against women who are more successful than we are, more forthright than we are, more comfortable with a sense of entitlement than we are…even more attractive than we are. We can even hold grudges against these women beyond their actual presence in our life.

For instance, a self-acknowledged fan of the Inner Bitch once gleefully recounted the life history of her high school nemesis. "Oh, she was such a bitch! She was the captain of the cheerleader team and she was just so cute and perky and now she's a hairdresser," this woman crowed, as if hairdressers weren't among the most powerful people in the world. (Admit it; we live in fear of the dreaded "bad haircut.") More to the point, as if being perky, cute, and captain of the cheerleader team—all incredibly powerful things in your average high school—was a punishable offense that bitch had nearly gotten away with.

While we'll admit that we have, on occasion, resorted to bitchy behavior ourselves, it's only because our hands were forced. In our more candid moments, we'll talk about our bitchiness with gleeful pride. Because, let's face it, there have been times in all our lives when being a bitch was fun. We all know it's true.

But ask us if we consider ourselves bitches and we will say no. Oh no, no, no, no, NO! We consider ourselves Nice Girls who are occasionally backed against the wall and must defend ourselves by acting like bitches. It's one thing to indulge ourselves in a little prickly behavior now and then. It's even okay to celebrate our strength and power. It's quite another to accept a vision of ourselves as strong, powerful, and—egads!—demanding women who expect more from life's banquet than a few little crumbs and are willing to put their expectations out there for the whole world to see. It's "those other women" who really are bitches. You know who they are.

Again, I don't think so.

In fact, I think that this dynamic carries in it the seeds of divisiveness. A dirty little secret is that Toxic Niceness works best when we are set apart from one another, when we are divided and disrespect each other. Because who knows what kind of earth-shattering changes might happen if women actually supported one another?

The bitches might take over the whole world.

IF I'VE GOT THE NAME, I WANT THE GAME

Any woman who succeeds at anything is going to be called a bitch. Madonna? Bitch. Hillary Clinton? Bitch. Martha Stewart? Bitch. Barbra Streisand? Bitch. The list goes on and on and on and…

The point is that since we can't avoid it, why don't we embrace it? We've all had this experience: at some point in time, in front of other people, we say what we really think about some issue or person or what-have-you. At some later point in time, someone tells us that, "So-and-so really thought you were a bitch." (If it hasn't happened yet, just keep talking—it will.)

Most of us make sure to be particularly nice to old so-and-so next time we see them. We may even go out of our way to prove that perceiving us as a bitch is not only erroneous, but downright unfair. Or we explain away all the reasons we said whatever it was we said. "I was under a lot of stress last time we met," or, "Gosh, I don't know what came over me!" Or even, "It must have been the hormones."

We retreat.

What if we responded by sending so-and-so a thank-you bouquet with a little card that said, "I really appreciate your recognition of my Inner Bitch."

What would happen if we stopped being afraid of this one little word?

Another point that must be made, which requires a short foray into rhetoric: what do we call a man who speaks up for himself, a man who is demanding of himself and those around him, a man who behaves as any self-respecting bitch would? A success.

Who is to blame for this?

Well, no one. Maybe everyone. One point about the Inner Bitch is so important, however, that it must be stated in no uncertain terms:

THE INNER BITCH IS NOT ABOUT BLAME

The Inner Bitch simply is, just as the sky is simply the sky, and dishes, once dirty, must be washed. There is no need to point a finger at anyone. Nor is there a reason to apologize for being in touch with Her. After all, She is the part of us that knows what we really care about and want.

She knows that we take pride in our work and that we hold ourselves and others to a certain standard.

She knows that we want our lovers to please us sexually (more about this later).

She knows that we want our friend, The Bride, to understand that wearing taffeta after the age of twelve is embarrassing.

She knows that we want the world to take the measure of our accomplishments, not of our bodies. She knows that we want to be able to say what we know, without being called names.

As long as we deny that the Inner Bitch is part of us, as long as we succumb to Toxic Niceness, we will not get what we want. We will not get what we need. And none of us will really get what is good for all of us.

"REAL SISTERHOOD [IS]...
A BUNCH OF DAMES IN
BATHROBES THROWING
BACK M&MS AND MAKING
EACH OTHER LAUGH."

—MAXINE WILKIE

can we talk!

It doesn't really get any better than this: a bunch of women gathered together with time to talk. And what do we women do when we talk? We get to the bottom of things. It's beautiful.

We start in adolescence, when we struggle with everything. That's when we discover how insightful our friends are, how well they understand everything.

They sympathize with us about the unreasonable curfew, and the impossible history exam; they commiserate with us over the painful braces, the boy who doesn't call, and the new shirt that shrinks in the wash; and they swoon with us over our teen idols.

Once we have recovered from our teens (and most of us do, eventually), we are able to form strong, valuable friendships with other women. Our best friendships are ones in which we meet each other head on with our Inner Bitch.

As my friends and I struggle with our tendencies toward Toxic Niceness, our Inner Bitch compels us to set boundaries that keep our friendships healthy. Emotional blackmail? Betraying secrets? Nasty gossip?

I don't think so.

FRIENDS INDEED

Is it easy for two or more women who are in touch with their Inner Bitches to be friends? I don't think so, but it's certainly more meaningful than those relationships that are based on Toxic Niceness.

The rules that govern relationships between women are so complex that the Gordian knot looks like a child's puzzle in comparison. But it's this complexity that makes friendships of this sort so very rewarding.

Our friends who are in touch with their Inner Bitch are often the most supportive, the ones to whom we turn when we feel our resolve begin to slip in the face of unreasonable bosses and impossible deadlines, the lover who suddenly stops calling, the expensive earring lost. They are the ones who remind us of the importance of our dreams and aspirations, quietly or loudly urging us forward when the path seems too steep or long.

The primary element of women's bonding is love. If we didn't love one another, we wouldn't bother telling the truth. We'd just let one another lurch from one delusion to the next, gathering up enough experience to make blues singers of all of us.

The beauty of getting in touch with our Inner Bitch is that we can then hear our own voices. The Inner Bitch knows what She knows. And She's not afraid to say it. But it is up to us to listen. The fact is, after we have had enough experience with jive, we can see it coming. And we can sometimes pull a good friend out of harm's way.

For example, when our friend's Joe breaks her heart by running off to help his buddy start a business in Hawaii, do we point out that we'd told her so? Of course not. Being in touch with our Inner Bitch requires sensitivity.

> Her: "I can't believe he left me! And to live someplace that's warm all year, too! Maybe I should follow him."

> You: "Do you know how many toxic insects there are in Hawaii?"

Then we make sure to get together often to watch movies like *Thelma and Louise* or *The Lion in Winter* and order take-out food (anything but poi). Eventually we move on to extremely romantic films set in locations like Alaska, taking care to point out how sexy it is to find out exactly what's under that parka.

SYLVIA   **by Nicole Hollander**

"Love me in
full Being."

—ELIZABETH BARRETT BROWNING

CHaPTeR FIVe

THe BITCH IN BeD

Well, the Bitch in love—really. How can we maintain the Inner Bitch in that most heady arena of life: romance? If it is true that what we seek from our love partners is intimacy, then it is vital that said partners be aware of our Inner Bitch. We can't be intimate with anyone who doesn't know and respect every aspect of our personality.

Let's face it, romance is where Toxic Niceness is most prevalent. And where it is most dangerous, too.

Because many of us are afraid that if the ones we love really knew us, they wouldn't want anything to do with us. But if they don't know the real us, we live in fear that they will no longer love us if we reveal ourselves to them. So we dedicate ourselves to being thoughtful, agreeable, helpful, sweet, nice, nice, nice.

Unfortunately, no one can pull this off for a lifetime. Eventually, Toxic Niceness is going to come to an end in the nastiest of ways.

It might happen when, for the ten thousandth time in a row, our beloved neglects to put in a new garbage bag after taking out the trash, which he always does just as we're beginning to make dinner and we really need to get rid of the chicken innards and-when-did-making-dinner-become-my-job-anyway?

It might happen while we're deciding which movie to see and we just will not subject ourselves to another action-packed extravaganza featuring an aging male star who is fated to end up with the beautiful starlet who's half his age.

It might happen when our beloved offers another "helpful" suggestion about our golf game, a situation at work, our workout or, perhaps, not actually eating the entire bag of M&Ms in one sitting (even though he knows what time of the month it is).

Whatever the precipitating event, we explode—years of being Nice are washed away in a stream of invectives, we end up in tears and, ultimately, feelings of incredible remorse that toss us back into the waiting arms of Toxic Niceness. And the pressure begins to build once more.

Golly, now there's a vicious cycle! Being in touch with our Inner Bitch leads the way out of that cycle.

THE TOXIC WAY TO INTIMACY

It usually starts with the first date. Here's a scenario in which Toxic Niceness is at work:

Prospective Love Partner: "I was thinking we should go see a movie."

Toxic Nice Girl: "Okay."

In reality, Toxic Nice Girl hates movies and would prefer to do something more interactive, like shoot pool. But she is unwilling to say so, for fear that her date will think she's too pushy, or too demanding, or...a bitch.

During that first date, Toxic Nice Girl will undoubtedly behave as if she is actually enjoying herself, when what she really wants is a chance to get to know this guy. She will also probably thank him for a wonderful time, all the while thinking, "If he really likes me, eventually we'll do what I want to do."

Of course, they never do. Toxic Nice Girl will continue to acquiesce until she feels she's in a powerful enough position to actually demand that she get her way, usually just after her wedding. At which point her partner will be justified in wondering, "What happened to the nice girl I fell in love with?" But that's another book. Really.

THE INNER BITCH WAY TO INTIMACY

How much simpler it is when we are fearless from the start. Watch this:

Him: "I was thinking we should go see a movie."

Inner Bitch Girl: "I'd like to get to know you better. How about we go shoot some pool?"

This way, the guy has a good idea of what she wants right from the start. And there is room to compromise. Inner Bitch Girl has suggested doing what she wants and left the door open for a counteroffer. This starts the prospective relationship off on an equal footing.

Of course, the man may not want to compromise. He may, indeed, be turned off by a woman who doesn't comply with every suggestion. That sort of guy will leave eventually. But that's okay, because we don't want a love partner like that, do we?

I don't think so!

Sex and The Inner Bitch

Okay. Take a deep breath.

This is, admittedly, one of the most sensitive areas of our lives when it comes to the Inner Bitch. Actually, sex is one of the most sensitive issues, period. Therefore, it follows that it is most important to be in touch with our Inner Bitch before we fall into bed with anyone. Here's why.

SELECTIVITY

Being in touch with our Inner Bitch ensures that we will carefully choose the people with whom we share our bodies.

There are loads of us who, in the interest of being nice, have ended up sleeping with people with whom we later realized we wouldn't even want to have a cup of coffee. (Come on, you know it's true!)

The justifications? "I didn't want to hurt his feelings." Or, "I don't know, it just happened."

No need to beat ourselves up over having done these things. But is it necessary to continue to do this?

I don't think so.

Orgasms

Toxic Niceness can be a serious impediment to sexual satisfaction. "I didn't want him to think I was unhappy," Toxic Nice Girl says, after months (or years) of unsatisfactory sex. Being in touch with our Inner Bitch ensures that we will have orgasms. Even with other people.

And we're not afraid to have them tell us what they want, either. Everyone wins when the Bitch is in bed.

Safe Sex

Being in touch with our Inner Bitch ensures that, having chosen carefully, we will not talk ourselves into believing that, by virtue of niceness, it would be impossible for our partner (or us) to have a sexually transmitted disease. Niceness does not immunize anyone.

Insisting on practicing safe sex may be difficult, but consider the alternatives. So, how does the Inner Bitch broach the subject? Forthrightly, that's how.

For example:

Everything is just right, the lights are low, music is playing softly, and you've spent the entire evening testing the waters, so to speak. You come up for air, gaze into each other's eyes. Neither of you wants to break the spell of the moment, but you know you must.

"Sweetheart," you say, "are there condoms in the house?"

"No, my love," he replies. "But you can trust me."

"I don't think so," you say, pulling yourself together.

If his response is, "No, but I'll run down to the all-night drugstore," by all means, offer to drive.

And remember, we are adults now. It's okay for us to carry condoms.

Maxine
What am I doing? I don't need four pieces of chocolate cake...
Am I eating to fill some INNER emptiness?
My hunger could all be EMOTIONAL!
It could be my HEART crying out for LOVE!
Love!
I can't feel WHOLE without LOVE!
Get real!
Or it could be my stomach crying out for chocolate cake...
I can't feel WHOLE without chocolate cake! Four slices minimum! With some peppermint ice cream on the side..
© 1992 Marian Henley

"THE EFFECT OF EATING TOO MUCH LETTUCE IS SOPORIFIC."

—BEATRIX POTTER

CHAPTER SIX

GLORIOUS FOOD

Q: "What does the Inner Bitch make for dinner?"
A: "A choice."

The Inner Bitch is a powerful ally to have in the ongoing struggle between our minds and our bodies. For example, my mind says, "Grains, veggies, fruit." My body tends to say, "Melted cheese, melted cheese, chocolate." What role does my Inner Bitch play in all this? Voice of reason, voice of stomach.

That's right; food is the one area where even the Inner Bitch plays both sides.

The difference is that being in touch with my Inner Bitch keeps the whole thing in perspective. She allows me to honor my food cravings while remembering to maintain good health.

Does this phrase sound familiar? "Oh, I've been really bad!"

Of course it does, and it's not sex we're talking about. No, we are almost always referring to something that we've eaten. Chocolate, perhaps; french fries; fettuccine Alfredo; if we consume anything beyond lettuce and a Diet Coke, we judge ourselves with the harshness of Calvinists. And usually condemn ourselves to several days of eating nothing but bottled spring water and the odd carrot or celery stick. This we refer to as "being good."

But the question must be posed: Is it good to be cranky and light-headed?

I don't think so!

How can we think and act in our best interest when we're obsessed with calorie counts, bathroom scales, and tape measures?

Back to Basics

Our Inner Bitch reminds us that food is basic to survival, not to mention peace of mind. Sometimes, food is just plain comforting. What could be better after a really wretched day than a big bowl of garlic mashed potatoes? Or an entire bag of peanut M&Ms—the one-pounder, not the single serving size? It may be that our Inner Bitch could have prevented us from having a wretched day in the first place, but once it's happened, our Inner Bitch knows that any means of saving a day from being a total wipeout is a good thing.

Food can also be an event, an opportunity to make contact with the important people in our lives.

Some of us find the process of getting and preparing food calming and creative. Some of us go to great lengths to avoid everything but its consumption. It doesn't really matter where you are on the spectrum, because the mechanics of food aren't the issue. What is the issue is that food must be dealt with. And our Inner Bitch allows us to make food arrangements that work for us.

When we are in touch with our Inner Bitch, we don't have to create a ten-course meal for in-laws who have never been kind to us, or for business associates who don't support us, or for friends with a tin palate.

Perhaps the most important point is this: our Inner Bitch takes food, and all the rituals surrounding food, seriously. But She is not taken in by the tyrannies of fashion. What does our Inner Bitch have to say about diets that require a grown woman to consume fewer calories than a two-year-old?

"I don't think so."

What is Her response to the expectation that all women—no matter what their natural body type—should wear clothing no larger than size twelve?

"I don't think so."

Our Inner Bitch sees the absurdity of trying to look like someone else, when each of us is already such a beauty.

"IT IS ONLY TRIFLES THAT IRRITATE MY NERVES."

—VICTORIA, QUEEN OF ENGLAND

CHAPTER SEVEN

DAILY LIFE

We may think of our Inner Bitch only in connection with special occasions, sort of like a party dress or lipstick. Our thoughts might go something like this: "I'll just save my Inner Bitch for when I really need Her. After all, I wouldn't want to wear Her out." As if the Inner Bitch were a pair of cheap shoes with flimsy soles. Could something this powerful be so fragile?

I don't think so.

The Inner Bitch is perfect for every occasion—casual, formal, private, or public—sort of like basic black. She is a vital part of our daily lives.

It is necessary, however, to practice discernment when utilizing Her power.

KNOWING THE DIFFERENCE

There are always going to be things about which we can do nothing—traffic, lines at the grocery store, increased activity on the surface of the Sun. Do we rant and rave at these things?

I don't think so.

We can take some comfort from the knowledge that we have no power over some situations—the Inner Bitch doesn't bother expending energy on things that are beyond Her control.

At the same time, it would take a saint not to react to the pressure caused by those things that are out of our control. And maybe not reacting is a sign of Toxic Niceness. Be that as it may, the important thing to remember is that the Inner Bitch can help us to respond—rather than react—to situations that are out of our control.

MaKING "I DON'T THINK SO" WORK FOR US

Take a typical day. We step out every morning to conduct our lives and something happens. Something always happens. We are waiting on line at the deli for our bagel (lightly toasted, with just a bit of cream cheese), and when the person behind the counter asks who is next, someone steps in front of us, saying, "I am," and begins ordering from a list—typed single-spaced on a sheet of legal paper.

We go shopping at the mall. As we enter the upscale anchor department store, we encounter the ubiquitous purveyor of perfumes standing at the ready with her atomizer and well-rehearsed spiel about how this scent will change our lives. "Would you care to experience Raison d'etre?" she asks.

Perhaps we encounter another driver in a parking lot. The type of encounter in which that driver backs into our passenger side. The impact of the collision dislodges the side-view mirror, an inconvenience that (according to the other driver) will have little impact on our lives. "The rearview mirror's all ya really need anyway, sweetie," he says.

To each of these situations we can respond, "I don't think so."

This takes some practice. At first, the prospect of a direct confrontation may fill us with dread. But practice does indeed make for proficiency. And most people respond rather well to hearing the Inner Bitch mantra spoken aloud.

"Excuse me," we say to the line cutter. "I don't think so. I believe I was here first."

"Raison d'etre? I don't think so." It may be necessary to shield ourselves in some way from the shower of perfume that inevitably follows fast on the heels of the offer.

"I don't think so. I want your insurance information," we say to our new buddy.

What can they say in response, really? Is anyone going to argue?

Well, certainly there is a percentage of the population who will argue. There are plenty of people who hurl themselves into a perfectly absurd defense of just the sort of indefensible behavior referred to here.

Do we shrink in the face of this phenomenon?

I don't think so.

The mantra of the Inner Bitch is especially helpful when we are presented with unreasonable estimates for minor car repairs, when we are asked to "please hold" for the umpteenth time, and when others attempt to bully us into doing things for them.

Indeed, the phrase, "I don't think so," becomes more powerful the more we say it.

SYLVIA

by Nicole Hollander

"A WOMAN'S PLACE IS IN THE HOUSE, THE SENATE, AND THE OVAL OFFICE."

—Anonymous

CHAPTER EIGHT

PERSONAL POLITICS

The major concern of our Inner Bitch is, naturally, our life. Just getting through the day takes so much energy that there's very little left over for anything else. Laundry? It has to get done, so we do it. Sleep? We'd die without it. Work? Well, our survival often depends on our ability to provide for ourselves. It's entirely understandable that most of us don't have much time to devote to politics. Besides, what does it really matter?

Well, let's take a look at this, shall we?

PART OF THE PROBLEM

If we continue to enter politics at the rate we have been, it will be three hundred years before there's an equal number of women and men in the U.S. Congress.

Who's going to write laws that are good for women? We already know the answer. In light of that answer, we really must do more.

"More?" you say.

Yes, I say. I'm not talking about taking on another activity, or running for Congress (or even the school board), or doing something that will tip us over into the exhaustion that threatens every one of us. I'm talking about using our Inner Bitch to make a better world.

Part of the Solution

The easiest thing to do is to vote with our dollars. That's right, don't buy those products whose advertising belittles women, insults us, or raises by another notch or two the already unrealistic standards to which we hold ourselves. This takes thought and awareness, and not much time. And if the stores we shop in don't carry products that please us, it's up to us to let them know that, until our needs are met, we'll shop elsewhere.

We can turn off the radio when the offensive disc jockey starts talking.

When there's a candidate worth supporting, we can actually go to one of those fund-raising cocktail parties and we can bring friends.

The next time some elected official who does not serve our needs (we know who they are) sends us a letter asking for money to run again, we can return the letter in the handy pre-addressed envelope with a note saying, "I don't think so. Not until I see some results from you. For now, I'm donating my money to Emily's List instead."

The message will be received. Think of it as taking part in a collective "I don't think so." Imagine the possibilities.

SHE'S
THE GAL WHO CANNOT ENJOY
THE SWEET TASTE OF SUCCESS.

"POWER CAN BE TAKEN,

BUT NOT GIVEN."

—GLORIA STEINEM

CHAPTER NINE

WORK FORCE

Work is what we do for money. Money in this society equals power. When we suffer from Toxic Niceness, we fear power. We think it is unattractive.

We may couch this belief in phrases like "Money's just not important to me," but it's really that we fear power. Which may explain why, when asked to work more without being paid more, we just say yes.

When we are in touch with our Inner Bitch, we are not afraid of power.

We welcome power.

We also welcome the responsibility that comes with power. We take pride in being good at what we do, and eagerly accept new challenges. We also welcome the money, understanding that it is a manifestation of the energy we put into our work.

We deserve all the rewards that our abilities have won us.

POWER

Power begets more power. And power can be used to make changes. Big changes. Little changes.

We all know that, but the question is, "How do we get power?"

Well, we can be certain no one will hand it to us. Therefore, perhaps the best idea is to make like Lenin, who said, "I saw power lying in the street and I picked it up." Look around. Power is at our feet, or maybe on the desk. It may take some looking, given the state of most desks, but we can find it. We see it every day when we open our eyes to it.

Pick it up!

"I don't recognize it," you say? Here are some traits of power that you may have overlooked:

Teamwork

Power is built on teamwork—think of the Sistine Chapel. Michelangelo may have been the brains of the operation, but I assure you he had plenty of hands in his atelier. Teams are built of individuals. The stronger the individuals, the stronger the team. Toxic Niceness teaches us that being part of a team means agreeing with everything everybody else says. In truth, being part of a team requires that we honestly assess each situation that faces the team and that we speak out about problems or issues.

imagination

Power comes from imagination. Nothing has ever been created without imagination. No problem has ever been surmounted without imagination. Our Inner Bitch not only puts us in touch with our imagination, She makes us willing to speak up about it. We may not always be right, but being right isn't really the point. Speaking up is. Our contribution may spark an idea in someone else, and that idea might lead to a solution or an invention.

Knowledge

Power is knowledge. And knowledge is power. Each individual has knowledge no one else has. Combining everyone's knowledge begets more knowledge, the way combining rice and beans begets more protein.

How it works

Every workplace depends on people working together toward a common goal, whether it's serving food, putting out a newspaper, practicing law, or whatever. The more power each individual brings to striving for the goal, the more likely it is to be attained.

Toxic Niceness drains us of power. This means that it also drains power from whatever work we do. We may believe that being nice will get people to do what we want them to do. Nothing could be farther from the truth.

Which is not to say that we need to shriek and demand and throw our weight around. No, no, no! Remember—being in touch with our Inner Bitch does not mean that we get to be abusive to anyone. It simply means that we know when to be firm, when to state our position and let it be known that we will act upon our convictions.

RHYMES WITH RICH

If it's true that you only start being called a bitch when you're successful, then we should embrace the opportunity to be called a bitch in the workplace.

Being called a bitch usually means that we are right or that we are insisting on excellence from others.

According to some people, use of the term "bitch" has grown in direct proportion to the number of women who have reached the top of their field.

How do we get to the top of our field? We do our job very well, thus advancing to the next level. This usually requires that we work with other people, eventually being in charge of what those other people do.

If we ask those who report to us to do their job well, and that means they have to work harder than they did before, they will probably call us a bitch.

If those people who report to us do not do their job and we take them to task for that, they will call us a bitch.

If we have taken those people to task and they still do not do their job, we will undoubtedly be more firm with them the second time we talk to them. They will definitely call us a bitch.

Good for them. Better for us.

Because what it really means is that we know our business. Here is a simple truth: no matter how nicely we ask, if we are the boss, we are the bitch.

What's the important part of that homily? We are the boss.

"WE DIE BY COMFORT AND LIVE BY CONFLICT."

—MAY SARTON

CHAPTER TEN

CLOSE ENCOUNTERS

It's bound to happen. And although it might sound to the uninitiated like a potential cataclysm, an encounter between two of us who are in touch with our Inner Bitch actually holds the possibility of greatness.

What could be better, after all, than the Inner Bitch doubled? Or tripled, quadrupled, increased exponentially?

Consider this: when two of us in touch with our Inner Bitch meet head on, it's magnetic. We either feel ourselves drawn to each other or we are repelled. Either way, the dynamic that's going on is this: we're recognizing each other's power.

We may not ever become friends with those women whose Inner Bitch we encounter, but that's beside the point. The important thing is, even if we have to agree to disagree, even if we just can't believe the tactics the other woman is using, even if we are filled with envy or some other base emotion, nine times out of ten, the other woman's Inner Bitch will evoke our respect and admiration.

It's better to recognize that confrontation can be exhilarating, that the process of facing off with someone who is as sure of her point of view as you are of yours is an opportunity to become more clear. A close encounter with someone else's Inner Bitch is nothing to fear, it's something to welcome.

Perhaps most importantly, there is the potential for great vitality in those interactions where our Inner Bitch meets Her match. It's easy to be with people who agree with us; it's comfortable and dulls our edges. This can be dangerous. Getting along with everyone in our lives gets to be a habit again and Play Nicely gets a grip on us, beginning the spiral back into Toxic Niceness. Next thing we know, we're apologizing for everything, sitting home on Saturday nights waiting for the phone to ring, and eating the entire cake.

Is this what we want?

I don't think so.

"I am in the world to change the world."

—MURIEL RUKEYSER

THE BITCH IN EVERYWOMAN

The Inner Bitch manifests Herself in many archetypes. At different moments, your own Inner Bitch may resemble any one of these icons of female power.

KARA

The Valkyrie swan queen. Kara overwhelmed her enemies using only the sound of her voice. A bitch to be reckoned with, especially on the phone. She also tells it like it is to her best friends.

LILITH

Lilith was to be Adam's first wife, but she took one look at him and said, "I don't think so." So off she flew to the banks of the Red Sea, where she spent her days coupling with whomever pleased her, giving birth to hundreds of children every day. Needless to say, with that level of fecundity, some of Lilith's DNA has got to be coursing through each of us.

CATHERINE DE MEDICI

When she married one of those Kings Louis of France, Catherine brought eighteen of her favorite Italian cooks with her. Can you imagine the leftovers? And her home was her castle: she insisted everyone at court use forks to pick up their food, instead of using their fingers. Yes, Mom.

KATHARINE HEPBURN

I refer here to the public persona, not the private person who slept on the floor outside Spencer Tracey's room. Strong, sassy, and ultra-dignified. Never knew that women were supposed to be the inferior sex. Next time you encounter a nasty salesperson, be Katharine Hepburn.

LYSISTRATA

A well-known Greek organizer. Persuaded the women of her city-state to withhold sex until the men gave up their most ridiculous war. The key here is that Lys banded together with other like-minded women. Imagine what we could do with the U.S. Congress…

To bolster your courage as you express that power-packed phrase, "I don't think so," call upon any one of these great role models, any time.

"MACHO DOES NOT PROVE MUCHO."

—ZSA ZSA GABOR

...AND THE MEN WHO LOVE HER

Just for the record, the idea that we women who are in touch with our Inner Bitch hate men, or wish we were men, or want to be like men, can be summed up with one word—SILLY. I just had to make that point.

This chapter is dedicated to the men who really admire the women they know who are in touch with their Inner Bitch. We all know men like this—they usually live with our friends. Oh, okay, maybe you actually live with a man like this. I do.

The point is, there's a name for men like this—Prince (as in, "a Prince among men").

A Prince understands what the Inner Bitch is all about. He gets it.

A PRINCE IS NOT A WIMP

Wimps are those guys who believe that machismo is the highest manifestation of male energy. They are the men who stand us up. They are the guys who keep dropping the age limit on whom they'll date, until their daughters and their girlfriends are the same age. They're the guys who won't work for a female boss.

A Prince is a real man, i.e., a real human being.

WHO IS A PRINCE?

Here's how to recognize a Prince:

- A Prince really does take full responsibility for his share of raising the kids;
- A Prince understands why those ads for beer are offensive (you know the ones I mean);
- A Prince never takes it for granted that we'll do all the cooking;
- A Prince does not assume that we can't change a flat tire;
- A Prince offers encouragement, rather than advice;
- A Prince knows what he knows. And, at the same time, he knows what he doesn't know. He doesn't bluster his way through a situation with ever-deepening b.s. In fact, a Prince has a good grasp on just how attractive it really is to be able to say, "I don't know."

WHERE DID HE COME FROM?

Well, if we have an Inner Bitch who is a natural part of us, it must follow that there is also an Inner Prince.

Just as most women have been trained in the ways of Toxic Niceness, men have been trained in the ways of whatever it is they're suffering from. There are plenty of names for it; pick one. Chances are, if you've done your Inner Bitch homework, you won't need to be cruel about it. The point is to understand the dynamic at work here: men have been taught behaviors that probably run counter to their true natures.

NaTURE VS. NURTURE

My experience has been that it takes a lot of work for a man to become a Prince, but that the basic stuff is there all along.

And try this one on for size: even the wimpiest, most macho man has the capacity to become a Prince.

ASSESSING THE PRINCE QUOTIENT (PQ)

I used to think that men were going to take the following test themselves. Now I understand that we must administer the test ourselves, preferably at an early stage in a relationship. A word of caution, however: don't try to do this during any major sports event, right before you leave for a party or family gathering, just after making love, too early in the morning, too late at night, too soon after getting home from work…all of which leaves a window of opportunity starting at about 12:30 on Saturday afternoon and ending at 12:45 the same day. Here goes:

1. Women like to be called "girls."

   Agree/Disagree

2. When a woman is assertive, I think of her as a bitch.

   Agree/Disagree

3. When I am going somewhere with a woman in a car, I drive.

   Always/Most of the time/Seldom/Some of the time/Whose car are we taking?

4. I know how to do laundry and iron.

   True/False/Why bother? My mom does my laundry.

5. I had an emotional reaction to the movie *Field of Dreams*.

   True/False/Never saw it

INTERPRETING THE ANSWERS

Question 1

If you answered "Agree" and you are under the age of 65, it's a safe bet that you are not a full-fledged Prince. (-10 points, seniors get a 0)

However, if you based your answer on the fact that your mom and her friends like to be called girls, this reveals a level of sensitivity that implies Princeness. (+2 points)

If you answered "Disagree," take a moment to reflect on why you chose that response. Is it because women have corrected you for calling them girls? (+2 points)

Or was your answer based on thoughts you've had about the importance of language, and calling women girls is not only inaccurate, but insulting? (+10 points)

Question 2

If you agreed, define "assertive." (-10 points if your definitions for men and women are different)

If you disagreed, take +10 points.

Question 3

"Whose car are we taking?" is the question a Prince would ask. (+10)

"Seldom" indicates Princeness only if you own a car. (+7 if you own a car, -10 if you don't)

"Some of the time" seems equitable. (+5)

"Most of the time" may imply that you either drive a large car (conducive to carrying many people or things), or that you have a great car that everyone wants to ride in. (0 points) It may also mean that most of your friends don't own cars. Then you are generous to always drive them around, and we hope your friends pay for gas. (+10)

If your answer was "Always," we really do have to look at the reasons why that would be the case. But it doesn't look good for your Prince Quotient. (-10)

Question 4

Okay, this was a sort of trick question, and we won't add or subtract any points for it; I actually don't know how to do laundry. And I'm hopeless at ironing. We threw this on in to see if anyone was paying attention. Of course, if you're in junior high and your mom does all your laundry, that's just fine. No matter what answer you gave, take 0 points.

Question 5

Another trick question—everyone had an emotional reaction to that movie! "Emotional reaction," after all, covers quite a lot of territory. (0 points; it doesn't matter if you cried or not.) If you didn't see it, you are excused and may take an extra 2 points.

SCORING:
If your score was 32 points, you are a full-blown, totally-in-touch Prince.

If your score was 29, you have a high PQ.

19–21 is medium range PQ.

A score of -32 shows a very low PQ. The fact that you took this quiz, however, is a hopeful sign, because awareness is the first step. Don't despair, there is no such thing as a hopeless case. You can improve your PQ.

GETTING IN TOUCH WITH YOUR INNER PRINCE

All the things in this book that apply to women getting in touch with our Inner Bitch also apply to men becoming a Prince. To break it down for you:

1. When you sense b.s., don't explain it away—call it as you see it. Even (or maybe particularly) when it is your own b.s.

2. If the desire to act like a wimp is overwhelming, just say to yourself, "I don't think so. Get a grip, fella." This works very well, because it bears a striking resemblance to taking the time to respond carefully.

3. Learn the difference between being kind and being patronizing. For example, it is kind to say, "May I help?" when you see someone struggling to get something done—like putting two small children to bed. It is patronizing to say, "Y'know, when I put

them to bed, I just tuck them in and turn out the light."

4. Turn up the volume on your internal Prince voice. It's been there all along, whispering to you things like, "It really is okay to want to spend time with my kids."

Note: A father spending time with his kids is parenting, not baby-sitting.

5. Recognize that your Inner Prince and my Inner Bitch meet on solid and very even ground.

Solid, even ground is a terrific base upon which to build.

"SUCCESS BREEDS CONFIDENCE."

—BERYL MARKHAM

THE TEN-MINUTE BITCH

These are little things we can do during the day to sharpen reflexes dulled by immersion in Toxic Niceness. As is the case with any sort of exercise, the more we do them, the easier they are. Consider these to be basic training.

THE EYE-TO-EYE EXERCISE

Stand before a mirror and look yourself in the eye. Think of the last time someone requested something of you that was absurd. For most of us, that would have been within the past twenty-four hours. Something really silly, like the time your cousin went to India for a month for intensive meditation and asked you to feed her cats every day. In spite of the fact that this required you to drive for an hour, you said yes, didn't you?

Imagine she is asking you to do it again. Hear her voice, see her face. Now smile and say, "I don't think so, Cousin Menakshi."

This is especially instructive, because as you remember these absurd requests (whether or not you agreed to them), a pattern may become clear to you. These are the areas where Toxic Niceness is particularly strong in your life. This is important information to have, because awareness is the first step in eradicating unwelcome behaviors.

VOTING WITH OUR POCKETBOOKS

Gather together every magazine you have lying around the house. Go through them page by page and rip out any advertisement that offends you. You don't have to justify your being offended, just recognize it. Once you have all those pages gathered (there will probably be a large pile), make a list of the companies behind them and send them an email telling them you won't buy their products until they stop using offensive ads. Then follow through—don't buy their products. Do we want to give those companies our money? I don't think so. Eventually, they will get the message.

I LOVE MYSELF; I THINK I'M GRAND

You know those diet books and articles that you've accumulated over the years? Destroy them.

Each day, rip out a few pages to burn in the sink as you say, "I am an adult. I choose what I eat." If you don't think you look great, choose to take reasonable action.

We all have enough information about how our bodies work; use whatever works for you. Most important, just say, "I don't think so," to the unrealistic ideal everyone else sets for us. Women are supposed to look like people, not scarecrows.

Ten Most Wanted

Make a list of all the people who have taken advantage of your immersion in Toxic Niceness. It doesn't matter if they were manipulative, malicious, or mean-spirited, because their behavior is not the point—yours is. Once a week, pick one of those people and outline for yourself the situation that occurred with that person.

Now, write it the way you wish it had happened, paying specific attention to your behavior. Don't be afraid; no one else is ever going to see this. The point is this: by rewriting our personal history, we are able to change our present and our future. Knowing what we wish we had done in a situation prepares us for the next time. And there is always a next time.

Coach One Another

This can be done in person, over the phone, by email—however it works for you. When faced with a situation that kicks you into High Toxicity, reach out to your Inner Bitch Coach as soon as possible. Explain the situation and ask for guidance. Because our friends want what's best for us and can usually see our lives more clearly than we can, they will be able to coach us back to the Inner Bitch way of doing things. For example, here's how some friends of mine used coaching to get one of them out of a situation Toxic Niceness had gotten her into:

Friend A: "My coworker has been taking the train to work every day, which takes over an hour, then she has to take the bus from the station to the office, which adds a half hour. I offered her a ride, so she's been taking the train to the station in my town and I drive us both to work. The problem is, she's a talker and conversation is the last thing I want in the morning. Plus, she shows up at my desk at the same time every evening, with her coat on and says, 'Ready?' I just can't take it anymore. I love my commuting time, it's the only time I have completely to myself. What do I tell her?"

Friend B: "Tell her your situation has changed and you won't be able to drive her to work any more."

Friend A: "What if she asks what's changed?"

Friend B: "Tell her you'd really rather not get into that. The truth is, what's changed is your realization that you want that time to yourself and you don't have to explain that to anyone."

THE POWER LULLABY

I don't know about you, but the time I spend in bed just before sleep has always been a time of reflection for me. It used to work this way: I'd lie there thinking about all the awful things I'd done, starting when I was in preschool. And I'd beat myself up about those things. In fact, I'd get so upset with myself that I couldn't fall asleep for hours, because one thing led to another and by the time I was drained enough to fall asleep, it was time to get up. Needless to say, I wasn't at my best.

I believe I have found a better way to deal with this reflective time. I think about all the things I have done right in my life. All those times I paid attention to my Inner Bitch, and the times I've pulled myself out of a spiral into Toxic Niceness. I fall asleep with a smile on my face. And when I wake up in the morning, I feel powerful.

Just thought I'd share this with you.

ABOUT THE AUTHOR

Elizabeth Hilts lives in Connecticut, where she continues to evolve and grow in her bitchiness.

Since the first edition of *Getting In Touch With Your Inner Bitch* was published, Elizabeth has had the opportunity to share her experience and views with women (and men) all around the world. One of her proudest moments was learning that Rush Limbaugh had dubbed her a "radical feminist theorist," a title she is considering adding to her business card.

Elizabeth would like to see this book reach every woman who wants to laugh out loud and speak her mind.

THE INNER BITCH GUIDE TO MEN,
RELATIONSHIPS, DATING, ETC.

Your Inner Bitch, that integral, powerful part of you, is essential when you're falling in love (and even more essential when you're falling out of love).

Looking for romance? Looking for a date? Looking for a relationship?

Let your Inner Bitch be your guide.

"REMEMBER, LUST MAKES YOU STUPID."
—NICOLE HOLLANDER

The Inner Bitch Guide to Men, Relationships, Dating, Etc., is available at bookstores everywhere, or by calling 800-727-8866.